North American

# INDIAN NATIONS

## NATIVE PEOPLES
### of the
# ARCTIC

### Stuart A. Kallen

LERNER PUBLICATIONS ◆ MINNEAPOLIS

The editors would like to note that we have made every effort to work with consultants from various nations, as well as fact-checkers, to ensure that the content in this series is accurate and appropriate. In addition to this title, we encourage readers to seek out content produced by the nations themselves online and in print.

Consultant: Dalee Sambo Dorough, assistant professor, Political Science, University of Alaska Anchorage; member of the United Nations Permanent Forum on Indigenous Issues (Inuit)

Lerner Publications Company
A division of Lerner Publishing Group, Inc.
241 First Avenue North
Minneapolis, MN 55401 USA

For reading levels and more information, look up this title at www.lernerbooks.com.

Main body text set in Rockwell Std Light 12/16.
Typeface provided by Monotype Typography.

Library of Congress Cataloging-in-Publication Data

Names: Kallen, Stuart A., 1955– author.
Title: Native peoples of the Arctic / by Stuart A. Kallen.
Description: Minneapolis : Lerner Publications, 2017. | Series: North American indian
   nations | Includes bibliographical references and index.
Identifiers: LCCN 2015044353 (print) | LCCN 2015051369 (ebook) | ISBN 9781467779371
   (lb : alk. paper) | ISBN 9781512412437 (pb : alk. paper) | ISBN 9781512410761 (eb pdf)
Subjects: LCSH: Inuit—Arctic regions—History—Juvenile literature. | Inuit—Arctic regions—
   Social life and customs—Juvenile literature. | Indians of North America—Arctic regions—
   History—Juvenile literature. | Indians of North America—Arctic regions—Social life and
   customs—Juvenile literature.
Classification: LCC E99.E7 K126 2017 (print) | LCC E99.E7 (ebook) |
   DDC 970.004/9712—dc23

LC record available at http://lccn.loc.gov/2015044353

Manufactured in the United States of America
1-37528-18673-3/10/2016

# CONTENTS

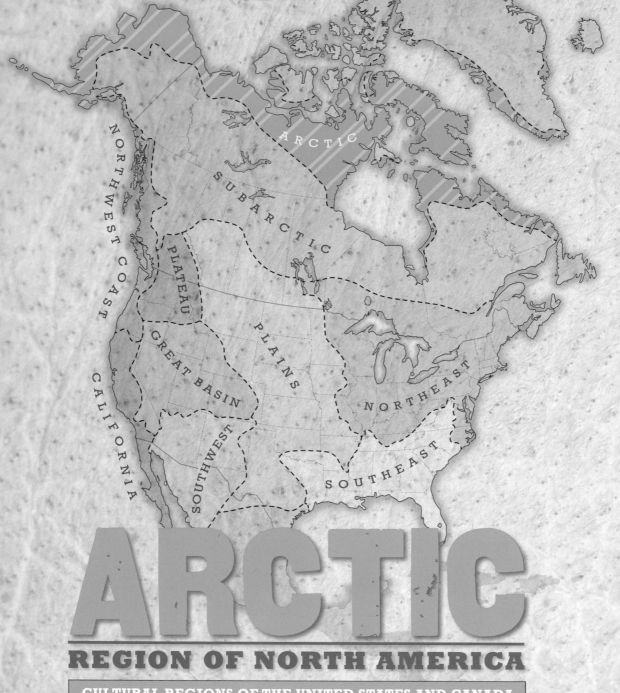

ARCTIC

A R C T I C

SUBARCTIC

NORTHWEST COAST

PLATEAU

GREAT BASIN

CALIFORNIA

PLAINS

SOUTHWEST

NORTHEAST

SOUTHEAST

# ARCTIC

## REGION OF NORTH AMERICA

### CULTURAL REGIONS OF THE UNITED STATES AND CANADA

| | | |
|---|---|---|
| Plateau | Southeast | Subarctic |
| Northwest Coast | Southwest | Arctic |
| California | Great Basin | Other |
| Plains | Northeast | |

- - - Cultural area border

——— International border

········· State/province border

# INTRODUCTION

**S**edna was a beautiful young woman who lived with her **father.** Many men in the village wanted to marry her. But Sedna would not get married. One day, a new hunter came to the village and asked to marry Sedna. She agreed. He took her back to his home, and she found that he was not a man at all! He was a bird. He couldn't hunt, and Sedna ate raw fish every day.

When Sedna's father came to visit, he saw that she was unhappy. He decided to take her home with him in his boat. But Sedna's husband found out and flew after them. He started a big storm. Sedna's father was afraid. He pushed Sedna out of the boat. She held on to the side of the boat. So Sedna's father chopped off her fingers, one by one. They fell into the sea and became fish, seals, walruses, and whales.

Sedna became the goddess of the sea. She sits at the bottom of the ocean. If she is happy with the people, she gives them lots of sea animals to hunt. But if she is unhappy, she makes sure the hunters are unlucky.

The story of Sedna is one of the most important stories of the Inuit (IN-yoo-it), the people who call the Arctic home and who depend on seals and whales for survival. There are several different versions of this story. In all of them, Sedna rules the sea

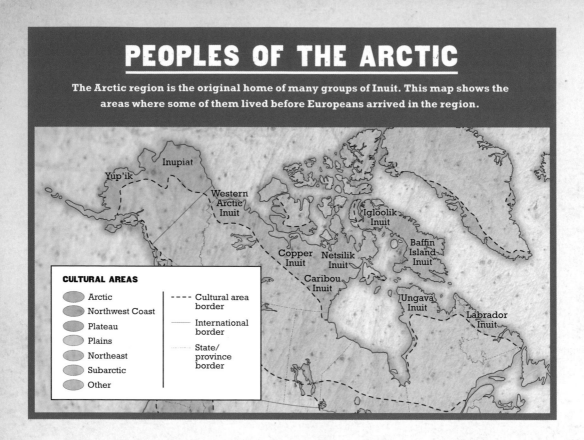

# PEOPLES OF THE ARCTIC

The Arctic region is the original home of many groups of Inuit. This map shows the areas where some of them lived before Europeans arrived in the region.

Inupiat

Yup'ik

Western Arctic Inuit

Igloolik Inuit

Copper Inuit

Netsilik Inuit

Baffin Island Inuit

Caribou Inuit

Ungava Inuit

Labrador Inuit

**CULTURAL AREAS**

- Arctic
- Northwest Coast
- Plateau
- Plains
- Northeast
- Subarctic
- Other

- - - - Cultural area border
——— International border
········· State/province border

and her fingers become the creatures of the sea. The Inuit have great respect for Sedna and the sea. Whenever they hunt a seal, they give thanks to Sedna.

## A Frozen Land

About 1,600 miles (2,575 kilometers) south of the North Pole, there is an imaginary east-west line around Earth. This is called the Arctic Circle. The region above that circle is called the Arctic. It is one of the harshest environments on Earth.

The Arctic has long been home to thousands of indigenous peoples. The North American part of the region covers parts of northern Alaska; Yukon Territory, the Northwest Territories, Nunavut, Quebec, and Labrador in Canada; and Greenland.

Throughout Alaska, Canada, and Greenland, most indigenous peoples are Inuit. Inuit are distinct from all other American Indian nations. In Canada, Inuit have been divided into eight groups. They are the Labrador, Ungava (uhn-GAH-vah), Baffin Island, Igloolik (IH-gloo-lick), Caribou, Netsilik (neh-sihl-leek), Copper, and Western Arctic Inuit. Though the term Eskimo (ES-kih-moh) is falling out of usage, in Alaska it is sometimes used to describe both the Yup'ik (YOO-puhk) and Iñupiat (in-YOO-pee-aht). Their relations, the Aleut (AH-lee-yoot), also live in the southern part of this region. The term Aleut refers to both the Alutiiq (ah-LOO-tick) and Unangax (uhn-AIN-gax) peoples in Alaska.

The Arctic is one of the harshest environments on Earth. The sun does not set from May to August, and summers are so cold that there can still be ice and snow in June.

The Inuit and Aleut groups all speak different dialects of the Eskimo-Aleut language family. This language family includes many dialects of Inuit, Yup'ik, and Aleut languages. Across the Arctic region, there are many different languages, but they are all related. The closer Inuit groups live to one another, the more similar their languages are.

## Peoples of the North

Inuit arrived in Alaska about eleven thousand years ago. They spread to the Canadian Arctic about four thousand years ago. They then also spread to Greenland. Inuit hunted and fished for food and made clothes from sealskins and caribou skins. They traveled across the ice with dogsleds and paddled across open water in kayaks. After long, cold days of work, Inuit had

Inuit often traveled over the ice using sleds and teams of Arctic dogs.

Many people in the Arctic use snowmobiles to get around, like these people in the Arctic city of Iqaluit, Nunavut.

fun. They held contests and wrestling matches to develop endurance. And they gathered to sing songs and tell stories.

About 160,000 Inuit still live in the Arctic. They continue to survive by hunting and fishing. But like other North Americans, Inuit travel in airplanes, motorboats, cars, snowmobiles, and all-terrain vehicles. They live in houses, watch television, and buy things on the Internet.

Inuit learned to live on the frozen tundra and sea ice. They survived howling winds, blowing snow, and deadly cold. They may live in one of the coldest places on Earth, but Inuit continue to thrive in the Arctic region near the very top of Earth.

# CHAPTER 1

# SURVIVAL
## AGAINST THE ODDS

**L**ife in the Arctic is generally divided into two seasons, winter and summer. Arctic summers are short. But it is so cold that there can still be snow in June. And the sun does not set from May to August. A thick layer of soil stays frozen all year long. This is called permafrost. Arctic winters are long, dark, and cold. In some areas, the sun does not rise from November to January.

For thousands of years, Arctic life followed a basic pattern. In fall, the ice began to thicken. Then Inuit could go farther out over the water to hunt sea mammals, including seals, walruses, and whales. In spring, the ice broke up, and the ground thawed. This made it easier to travel inland to fish in lakes and rivers and hunt land animals such as caribou, musk oxen, deer, and moose. Some groups, such as the Caribou Inuit, lived farther inland. They relied on caribou almost all year. In the Aleutian Islands in Alaska, the open ocean water never completely froze. The Aleut survived on fish and seals all year.

Inuit hunters did not waste any part of an animal. The meat was eaten. The fat was cooked down into oil that was used as a dipping sauce. This oil was also used as fuel for heat, light, and cooking. Skins of caribou, seals, polar bears, and even birds and fish were made into clothing and boots. Large animal skins were made into tents and blankets. Bones, antlers, and ivory walrus tusks were sharpened to make needles, knives, and spearheads.

## Summer Fishing

In the summer, the Arctic waters were full of salmon, char, northern pike, and other fish. Inuit caught fish using nets made from tough animal tendons called sinew. After fish were caught, most were eaten fresh.

Extra fish were preserved. The easiest way to keep fish fresh was to use the permafrost as a natural freezer. Inuit would dig a hole in the frozen ground and bury the fish until it was needed. Fish could also be dried on racks in the sun or smoked over small fires in a smokehouse.

These children are standing under salmon that is being dried on a rack in the sun.

**M**any Inuit traveled on dogsleds pulled by huskies, malamutes, and other Arctic dog breeds. The sleds were made from animal bones and wood. They were large enough to carry families, food, and equipment. Dogsleds might carry hunters hundreds of miles along with meat, carcasses, furs, and bones.

During the summer, Inuit fished from the one-person boats they invented, called kayaks. These boats had wood or bone frames covered with sealskin. Boats called umiaks (OO-me-acks) were also made of wood, bone, and walrus skins. They could hold several people. Umiaks were used to move from camp to camp or to hunt larger sea mammals like whales. Women rowed the boats while the men steered using rudders.

**A group of Inuit traveling in kayaks**

## Hunting Skills

Entire villages worked together to hunt caribou. Hunters needed a number of skills to be successful. They made their own weapons such as spears, knives, and bows and arrows. Hunters also had to understand animal behavior. This helped them find caribou herds and predict how the animals would move and react.

Inuit prepared to hunt caribou by building long rock walls called cairns. The walls were angled and ended at a narrow opening that acted like a funnel. During a caribou hunt, the people gathered around a herd. Women and children screamed and beat stones together to scare the animals into running toward the cairn. Hunters waited at the other end. As the animals ran through the passage, the hunters killed the caribou.

Inuit butchered dead caribou in their camps. They removed the meat and buried it in the permafrost. They made the sinew into thread and rope. They stretched the skins on racks to dry in the sun for later use.

## Ringed Seals

During the winter, thick sheets of ice formed over the Arctic seas. Under the ice, the waters were full of ringed seals. Inuit hitched their dogs to dogsleds and traveled out onto the ice to hunt the seals.

Hunters needed to be very patient to hunt seals with spears. Seals can stay under water for a long time. But about every five to fifteen minutes, they need to rise to the surface to breathe. The seals clawed through the ice to create breathing holes. A thin layer of ice would form over these holes, making them hard to see. But the seals would return to the same holes to keep them from completely freezing over. Sometimes hunters used their

# WHAT IS AN INUKSHUK?

*I*nukshuk (in-UHK-shook) means "in the likeness of a human." It is a pile of stones built by Inuit to communicate with others. During a caribou hunt, hunters used the inukshuk to form the rock walls to direct the caribou to the hunters. Inuit would also build an inukshuk to mark places where they had saved food or where fishing was good. An inukshuk could point out directions or simply show that people had been in that place.

dogs to sniff out the breathing holes. Then they gathered around the holes and silently waited for seals to come up. They might wait an entire day to catch one seal. When the animals came into view, the hunters killed them.

## Arctic Shelters

Inuit hunted and fished over a large region. When they traveled, they made temporary shelters. These shelters were quick and easy to build. In the summer, they built tents. Very few plants and no trees grow in the Arctic, so the frames for their tents were made from driftwood logs that washed up on the shore. The logs were covered with skins of caribou or seals. Rocks were placed around the base of the tent to hold down the skins.

When winter came, Inuit families in the Canadian Arctic would build a sturdy house called a *qarmaq* (KUH-muhk) for protection from the cold. To build a qarmaq, they dug a hole in the ground that could be up to 6 feet (2 meters) deep. Then they built a frame of driftwood or large whalebones. They covered the frame with animal skins. A typical qarmaq could hold up to twenty people. The people used woven grass mats to divide the house into several rooms where individual families lived. Everyone shared a large common room. A village might also have one larger house for community meetings and celebrations.

Some Arctic nations, such as the Copper Inuit, spent all winter living in snowhouses on the ice while they hunted for seals. In other Inuit groups, a family might build temporary snowhouses. These houses, known as igloos, had thick walls made from blocks of snow. A skilled hunter could build a small igloo in about one hour. Several people worked together to make larger igloos. The hunters first cut several dozen snow and ice blocks from snowdrifts with bone knives and saws. They laid the

An Inuit family builds an igloo from blocks of snow.

# INUIT SHELTERS

| HOUSE | BUIDLING MATERIALS | HOW IT WAS USED |
|---|---|---|
| Tent | Driftwood, sinew, bone, skins, and rocks | Temporary shelter in summer during fishing and hunting trips |
| Igloo | Snow, ice, and skins | Winter shelter during whale, seal, and walrus hunts |
| Qarmaq | Driftwood, whalebone, skins, and grass mats | Permanent shelter for families in winter |

blocks in a circle. As they stacked the blocks, the hunters angled them inward. This created a domed shape.

When an igloo was finished, the hunter cut a doorway low in the wall. A tunnel of ice was built out from the door. This kept the wind from blowing into the igloo. An animal skin acted as a door.

## Fur Clothing

Men, women, and children of the Arctic all dressed similarly. Everyone wore two layers of clothing made from animal skins. The inner layer was a shirt and pair of pants. For extra warmth, this layer might be worn with the fur facing the body.

For an outer layer, Inuit wore mittens, another pair of pants, and a heavy knee-length parka with a hood. Women carried babies on their backs in a pouch called an *amaut*. This pouch was sewn as part of the backside of a parka. These parkas had an extra-large hood to cover and protect the babies.

Boots were made from waterproof sealskins. To avoid slipping on ice, the Arctic peoples invented spikes called crampons. These were made from jagged bits of bone or ivory. When they needed the spikes, people could tie them onto the bottoms of their boots.

Snow goggles were another Inuit invention. These goggles were made from a flat piece of wood or an antler. Two slits were made in the antler

Inuit mothers often carried their babies in a pouch called an amaut.

for the eyes. The goggles protected the eyes from the glare of the sun when it reflected off the snow. This glare could cause snow blindness, or sunburned eyes. The Aleut protected their eyes using hunting hats. These were made from wood that was curved into a long visor. The Aleut painted these hats and decorated them with bones and sea lion whiskers.

Inuit lived in harsh and dangerous conditions. But by using available resources, along with ingenuity, strength and creativity, they found ways to survive in their homelands in the Arctic.

# CHAPTER 2

# SOCIETY AND
# SPIRITUALITY

**Families were the most important piece of Arctic society.** A family was typically made up of five or six people. Six to ten families might live and hunt together. Females usually married around the age of thirteen. Males were usually several years older. In some communities, if a young man wanted to marry, his family would send gifts of furs to the girl's family. If the girl's family accepted the marriage proposal, the man would work for the family for a year. Often parents arranged their children's marriages. Some marriages were arranged when the children were babies. Sometimes the man would come to the girl's camp and pretend to steal her from her family. The newlywed couple usually lived with the husband's family.

## Boys and Girls

As in most cultures, children were highly valued in Inuit societies. Children brought joy to the community. They were also taught traditional skills so the family could survive. Many Inuit believed that children carried on the spirit of a deceased relative. Children were often named after a relative and treated with the same respect the relative deserved.

Boys as young as five traveled with their fathers and other men on hunting trips. The boys were given small bows and arrows to practice hunting small animals such as hare and birds. When a boy of twelve or thirteen killed his first seal or caribou, he was thought of as an adult.

Girls learned to sew and care for their younger siblings. During fishing trips, girls helped clean and smoke fish. After a hunt, girls worked with their mothers to skin and butcher animals and cook the meat.

Boys and girls were raised to respect their parents and grandparents. Everyone in the community honored elders for their knowledge. The elders knew about the past and their

An Inuit woman cooks a catch of crabs over a fire on the ice.

culture. They also knew the traditional languages and legends, which were not written down. Elders often told stories and gave advice to the younger generations.

## Spirits and Souls

Inuit believed that spirits existed in all living and nonliving things. In Inuktitut, a Canadian Inuit dialect, these spirits were called *anirniit.* When people or animals died, their spirits were said to live on in the spirit world. But the belief that all things have spirits could create problems. Inuit believed that killing an animal was the same as killing a human. So the spirit of an animal killed during a hunt could take revenge on a hunter. An angry spirit could cause starvation, sickness, and death.

To avoid upsetting the spirits, Inuit developed rules called taboos. Taboos were meant to calm spirits and keep them from becoming angry. One important taboo said that Inuit could not mix land animals with sea animals. For example, it was taboo to cook or eat caribou meat with seal meat. A knife used to butcher a whale had to be wrapped in sealskin, not caribou skin. And seal fur could not be used as trim on a caribou parka.

## Shamans and Magic

If a person broke a taboo or had other troubles with spirits, he or she could go to a shaman. Shamans were men and women who were said to have great powers. Shamans performed rituals to enter a dreamlike trance that allowed them to talk to the spirits. To help an unlucky hunter, the shaman might talk to the spirits of the caribou or seals. The spirit would tell the shaman the best time and place to hunt. The shamans could also perform rituals to control the weather or see into the future. The rituals involved chanting, singing, drumming, and dancing. They could last all night.

# A SHAMAN'S RATTLES AND DRUMS

**D**uring rituals, shamans used drums and rattles to communicate with the spirits. They shook their rattles loudly to call out to the spirits. The drum acted as the shaman's voice. Shamans might beat on a drum for hours to talk to the spirits.

Rattles were made from dried animal hide or wood filled with small stones. Drum frames were small wooden hoops. The drumhead came from a caribou skin or walrus stomach. The drum might be decorated with pictures of animals or symbols.

Shamans were also known as healers. They worked with souls and spirits to help the sick. Inuit believed that a person's soul could be stolen by an enemy or an evil spirit. When this happened, the person became very ill. To heal the person, the shaman searched for the person's soul in the spirit world. When the soul was found, it was returned to the person who lost it.

## Carving Art

Inuit have been making small sculptures of spirits for thousands of years. They made the carvings from stone, bone, antlers, and ivory. During the dark winter months, almost everyone learned to carve. They used blades and sharp needlelike picks made from bone. Most statues were small enough to fit into a person's hand. The carvings could be worn on a belt or on a string around the neck.

Inuit might carry carvings such as these for protection or to honor their ancestors.

Spirit statues were thought to have great powers. Shamans used them during rituals, and other people carried them for protection and luck. Hunters might wear a polar bear carving around the neck. This carving represented the spirit of the bear. It would protect them from a bear attack. They might also carry a small figure of a fish to have more success on a summer fishing trip. Carvers also honored their ancestors by cutting images of their faces into pieces of deer antlers.

## Masks and Dancing

Inuit artists made masks from driftwood, skins, bones, and feathers. The masks looked like important animals such as caribou, whales, or seals. The masks could also represent spirits or people. The masks were worn during religious holidays that happened every year in the first days of spring and the darkest nights of winter. People celebrated by drumming, dancing, singing, and storytelling.

Masked dancers might come together to tell the story of a hunt or a spiritual journey. Singers recited poems and stories while dancers acted out the words. Masks were also worn during rituals that followed the birth of a baby or a boy's first successful hunt. Shamans wore masks during rituals to help them communicate with the spirits.

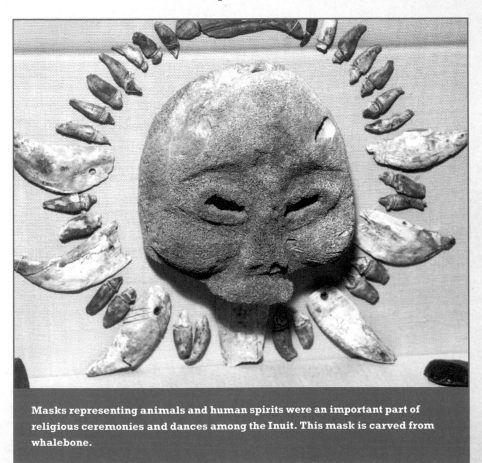

Masks representing animals and human spirits were an important part of religious ceremonies and dances among the Inuit. This mask is carved from whalebone.

# CHAPTER 3
# A CLASH OF CULTURES

**I**nuit lived off the land for thousands of years. They hunted and fished but killed only enough animals to survive. Food could be scarce, and life could be hard. But Inuit thrived in their traditional ways. That began to change after Europeans came to the Arctic in the eighteenth century.

## Otters, Whales, and Furs

The first lasting influence on native peoples of the Arctic occurred when Danish sea captain Vitus Bering came to Alaska in 1741. When Bering arrived in Alaska, he claimed the land for Russia. His crew found the water between Alaska and Russia, called the Bering Sea, filled with sea otters. Bering's crew sailed back to Russia with nine hundred sea otter pelts. The Russians wanted the pelts

Vitus Bering came to Alaska in 1741 and claimed the land for Russia.

Sea otters have soft, sleek fur that became very valuable for making coats and other expensive clothing.

to make capes, belts, and fur trim for coats. In Europe and Asia, the sea otter furs became very valuable. These pelts made high-quality clothing, and sea otter clothing became a sign of wealth. A single sea otter pelt was worth more than a sailor earned in a whole year.

In the nineteenth century, the whaling industry became popular around the world. Whale oil was burned in lanterns. A substance called baleen was used to make combs, whips, and other products. In the 1820s, whalers from Scotland and New England began traveling through the Arctic to hunt whales.

By the mid-nineteenth century, the whale population off the eastern coast of North America was dying out because so many people were hunting there. In 1848, a New York sea captain named Thomas Roys sailed to the Bering Sea. He was the first American whaler to come to the area. Roys found the sea filled with bowhead whales. These whales can be up to 60 feet (18 m) long and weigh up to 200,000 pounds (90,718 kilograms). The bowhead has up to six hundred baleen plates in its mouth.

Roys's discovery set off a whale rush. In 1852, more than two hundred whaling ships from the United States came to Arctic waters to hunt bowheads. The whalers arrived from the south in spring when the ice broke. Then they hunted whales for four months until the ice formed again.

Soon the whale population in the Arctic began to die out. The whaling ships left the Arctic. Whalers moved on to other trades. But the loss was devastating for Inuit. For generations, they had relied on the whale for food, clothing, and shelter. With whale numbers so low, Inuit no longer had enough food and materials to live.

**Thomas Roys found the Bering Sea full of giant bowhead whales like this one.**

# BLUBBER AND BALEEN

**I**n the nineteenth century, whales were at the center of an important American industry. The thick layer of fat, or blubber, beneath the skin of the whale provided oil. Along with fuel for lamps, whale oil was used to oil machines and turned into soap and paint.

Whales also provided baleen. Baleen is the name for the long, flexible plates found in the mouths of whales. Whales feed on tiny shrimp called krill. Baleen looks like a giant comb. It separates the krill from the seawater as the whales suck it into their mouths. Baleen was once used to make buggy whips, toys, combs, buttons, and corsets.

In the nineteenth century, Americans and Europeans began setting up trading posts across the Arctic. The largest trading company was the Hudson's Bay Company. By the end of the century, it had trading posts throughout the North American Arctic. As the whaling industry died down, the fur trade gained popularity. Inuit were very important for this industry. They hunted and trapped furs and received goods such as guns, tobacco, tea, sugar, and cloth in return.

With the growth of the fur trade, rifles replaced many traditional Arctic hunting methods. Guns allowed hunters to kill many more animals in a short time. Fur traders only wanted pelts. So the native peoples stopped using every part of the animal as they had for thousands of years. Animals were killed and skinned. Sometimes the carcasses were left to rot.

Caribou were some of the animals most affected by rifles. By the early twentieth century, the number of Arctic caribou

The Hudson's Bay Company was the largest trading company throughout the Arctic. This historic Hudson's Bay Company building is in Nunavut, Canada.

had gone from several million to about two hundred thousand. Hunters also wiped out large numbers of foxes, minks, and beavers.

## Cultural Loss

The arrival of Europeans in the Arctic changed cultural practices too. In Labrador, Europeans began setting up fishing and whaling posts in the middle of the sixteenth century. Inuit sometimes raided these posts for tools. But it wasn't until the eighteenth century that Europeans had much contact with the Labrador Inuit. In 1771, Moravian missionaries set up the Nain mission station. They began providing Inuit with tools and materials. The Moravians ended many aspects of Inuit religious culture, including dancing and drumming.

About a century after the Moravian missionaries came to Labrador, Anglican and Catholic missionaries began traveling to the Arctic. They wanted to convert Inuit to Christianity. The missionaries set up dozens of tiny churches near the trading posts.

Inuit spiritual practices clashed with Christianity. As the Moravians had in Labrador, these missionaries believed shamans were evil. They banned many traditional ceremonies. The missionaries also worked to end Inuit languages, drumming, and dancing.

The missionaries arrived when the fur trade was slowing down. Fashions were changing in Europe and America, and

Animal hides such as beaver, otter, rabbit, caribou, and seal were central to the Arctic fur trade.

fur clothing was going out of style. A financial crisis in Russia meant that people could no longer afford to buy fur clothing. By then, the lives of many Inuit had been dramatically changed. Ancient traditions were sometimes completely forgotten as people had come to rely on the trading industry to survive. In less than 150 years, Arctic culture had been radically transformed.

## Gold, Oil, and War

Life in the Arctic was even more radically transformed as the US and Canadian governments became interested in what lay to the north. The United States bought Alaska from Russia in 1867. That year, Canada became a country. A few years later, Canada began working to establish its ownership of the Arctic.

Prospectors pan the sand for gold on the beach of the Bering Strait at Nome, Alaska.

In the 1890s, gold was discovered in Nome, Alaska. Thousands of people moved north to search for riches. By 1900, Nome's population had grown to an estimated twenty thousand people. Inuit also moved to these areas to make money. Gold hunters called prospectors paid Inuit one hundred dollars a day to help in the gold fields. This was a fortune for most Inuit whose lives continued to revolve around hunting and fishing.

The gold rush did not last long. By 1910, most gold that could be easily found was gone. Large mining companies moved in to dig deep into the earth for gold. The US government became interested in the natural resources in Alaska. Schools, government offices, health clinics, and other sites were built with public funds.

Inuit children were traditionally taught important skills for surviving in the Arctic. But they had to stay in the settlements and go to schools that the government built. At Inuit schools, students had to give up many traditional customs. This meant dressing, speaking, and living like white Americans. Inuit students were not allowed to speak their native languages. Families stopped traveling long distances to hunt and fish so their children could go to school.

After World War II (1939–1945), Canada became more involved in its Arctic territories. The Canadian government built schools, hospitals, and airports. It forced Inuit to move into permanent villages. The government believed this would make it easier to help Inuit. But it also caused Inuit to lose many of their traditions and their land.

By the mid-twentieth century, modern inventions were changing the lives of people everywhere. In the Arctic, radios, movies, and televisions brought news of the outside world to people in remote areas. Gas heaters, cars, airplanes, and snowmobiles also made life easier for most. And Inuit were swept up in events happening far from their homes.

In the 1950s, Russia was part of the Soviet Union, a former nation made up of fifteen republics. The United States and the Soviet Union were engaged in what was called the Cold War (1945–1991). Each side built thousands of nuclear weapons and had the power to destroy the world many times over.

US military experts worried that Soviet bombers would fly over the Arctic to attack the United States. The Canadian and US governments worked together to build sixty radar stations across the Arctic Circle. The stations were known as the Distant Early Warning (DEW) Line. The DEW Line provided jobs for Inuit, but it was also built on their lands. Inuit communities were forced to move again.

**Aerial view of a Distant Early Warning Line station in Alaska**

After the construction of the DEW Line, oil was discovered in Alaska. Plans were made to build an oil pipeline from north to south across Alaska. The pipeline would pass through hundreds of miles of lands claimed by Alaska Natives. The Alaska Natives demanded that their land rights be recognized by the government. To settle these claims, Congress passed the Alaska Native Claims Settlement Act in 1971. The act confirmed native peoples' rights to land and gave them 44 million acres (17.8 million hectares) of land. The Alaska Natives were also paid nearly $1 billion to give up their claims to lands outside those given them under the act.

The settlement money was paid out over eleven years to native companies created by the act in more than two hundred villages. The funds were used to start mining, fishing, and timber businesses. These businesses helped lift many Alaska Natives out of poverty.

The Alaska Native Claims Settlement Act would begin a movement of Inuit, Aleut, and other Alaska Native peoples toward reclaiming their cultural heritage and working to get back everything that had been taken from them.

# CHAPTER 4

# OUR BEAUTIFUL
# LAND

**T**hroughout history, Inuit were largely ignored.
When Vitus Bering claimed land for Russia, he overlooked
the people already living on the land. When Americans and
Europeans hunted in the Arctic, they ignored that Inuit had
depended on those animals for thousands of years. When the
US and Canadian governments began building in the Arctic
territories, they moved Inuit with little concern for their overall
well-being. Many Inuit communities still have not been able to
entirely reclaim their cultures and traditions. But native peoples
and their governments have worked to give native peoples of the
Arctic a better life.

## Inuit Circumpolar Council

In the early 1970s, a few Inuit leaders recognized that for them
to be able to continue living in the Arctic, they would need to
organize themselves and speak up. They would need to work
together to protect themselves and their culture. One Inuit
from Alaska, Eben Hopson, held the first Inuit Circumpolar
Conference in Alaska in the summer of 1977.

From left, Inuit Circumpolar Council (ICC) Vice Chairman Aqqaluk Lynge, of Greenland; Chairman Jimmy Stotts, of Alaska; and Executive Council Member Violet Ford of Canada at a press conference in 2009

At that meeting, fifty-four Inuit from Canada, Alaska, and Greenland gathered to discuss politics, read poetry, and sing songs. They also started an organization to continue working together to promote Inuit rights in order to protect their culture. Several years later, Inuit from Russia also joined the organization.

The group still meets every four years to represent unity and promote the rights of the more than 160,000 Inuit living in the Arctic regions of the world.

## A New Territory

Around the same time as the Inuit Circumpolar Council was founded, Canadian Inuit were discussing their own land claims. A group of Inuit then known as the Inuit Tapirisat of Canada suggested that a new Inuit territory be created in Canada. More than twenty years later, in 1999, the Canadian

The flag of Nunavut was unveiled on April 1, 1999, at the official ceremony to inaugurate Nunavut in Iqaluit, Canada.

government declared Nunavut a new territory.

Nunavut means "our land" in Inuktitut. There, more than 80 percent of the population is Inuit. Most representatives in the Nunavut government are Inuit, and Inuit participate in all discussions about their lands and communities. They own and manage 136,000 square miles (352,239 sq. km) of Nunavut. And they receive money from the development of oil, gas, and mining activities in Nunavut.

Inuit in other regions of Canada have made similar agreements. After years of discussions in Labrador, the Labrador Inuit Land Claims Agreement was passed in 2005. This agreement recognized Labrador Inuit rights to land and

# NANOOK OF THE NORTH

In the twentieth century, few Americans knew much about life in the Arctic. What little they did know about Inuit life and culture came from a single man known as Nanook of the North. Nanook's real name was Allakariallak. He lived with his family in the Arctic region of northern Quebec, Canada.

In 1920, movie director Robert J. Flaherty filmed Nanook as he built an igloo, visited a trading post, and hunted a walrus with a harpoon. In 1922, the film was made into a silent movie called *Nanook of the North.* It was a huge box office success in the United States and around the world. The movie has since received criticism because it is not a true documentary. Some scenes were scripted and staged. It often did not accurately show how Inuit life was in the 1920s but tried instead to show how life had been before European contact. But critics at the time praised the movie, and Nanook painted an image of life in the Arctic that lasted with viewers for decades.

Allakariallak, the Inuit featured in *Nanook of the North,* a film depicting life in the Arctic

Climate change and melting ice are causing many problems and challenges for those living in the Arctic.

coastal waters. It also recognized the ability of Labrador Inuit to govern themselves. Inuit territory in Labrador became known as Nunatsiavut, meaning "our beautiful land."

## A Changing Climate

The money and land claims agreements that Inuit achieved have helped bring them stability and security. But life in these communities is not easy. People still struggle between living in their traditional ways and being part of Canada or the United States. Poverty is a problem in many rural and remote native communities. And living on the land is still hard. By the 1980s, more and more climate scientists were studying climate change. Global temperatures were rising due to the burning of oil, coal, and other fossil fuels. These dramatic changes in climate began to have an impact on Arctic communities, especially the Inuit.

In September 2015, Barack Obama became the first American president to visit the Arctic. President Obama flew into the tiny town of Kotzebue, Alaska, where he heard about the many problems caused by climate change. Inuit there told him that the caribou population has dropped by half in recent years. The spring seal hunt used to last three weeks. But in 2015, the

US president Barack Obama greets supporters gathered at the airport of an Arctic village on September 2, 2015, in Kotzebue, Alaska.

ice was too thin. The hunt lasted only three days. This is a huge problem in a region where a single seal can feed a large family for an entire winter. And this is just one example of the impact of climate change.

## Long-Term Survival

Throughout the Arctic, Inuit live like people in the rest of the world. They use the Internet and listen to satellite radio. They play organized sports in local schools, and they watch movies.

But many young Inuit are reviving ancient traditions. Some leave their homes in the spring and summer to set up hunting and fishing camps. Some young Labrador Inuit have learned the dances that missionaries ended so many years ago. The Arctic Winter Games are held every two years. Along with sports such

Two athletes compete in the head pull event in the Arctic Winter Games.

# ARCTIC POPULATIONS

| NATION | POPULATION |
|---|---|
| **Aleut** | 19,282 |
| **Inuit** (Canada) | 59,445 |
| **Inuit** (Greenland) | 50,000 |
| **Iñupiat** (Alaska) | 33,360 |
| **Yup'ik** (Alaska) | 33,889 |

*Census numbers according to most recent data from each country.

as curling, skiing, and hockey, there are traditional competitions to measure strength, flexibility, and endurance. There are cultural events such as throat singing and dancing too. The Inuit dialect Inuktitut is widely spoken throughout Nunavut. And the Aleut are working to pass on traditional languages and skills to the next generation. Young Inuit tell stories, create sculptures, make clothing from furs, and are reviving legendary dances as a form of storytelling. By doing so, they are ensuring the survival of their rich culture for generations to come.

# NOTABLE INUIT

### John Quniaq Baker

is a dog musher who races in the annual Iditarod Trail Sled Dog Race. Baker entered his first Iditarod race in 1996 and has been in every race since. He has achieved thirteen top ten finishes.

### William L. Hensley,

known as Iġġiagruk, is an Inuit leader, Alaska state senator, and founder of the Northwest Alaska Native Association (NANA). He also worked closely with the Alaska Federation of Natives (AFN). Throughout his career, Hensley has been involved in both environmental and land claims issues.

### Irene Bedard

is an award-winning actress who has played American Indians in many films. She was the voice of Pocahontas in the 1995 animated film *Pocahontas*. Bedard was nominated for a Golden Globe for her 1995 role in *Lakota Woman: Siege at Wounded Knee*.

### Annie Pootoogook

is a Canadian Inuit artist whose ink and crayon drawings depict her life and her community. Pootoogook's drawings show traditional work such as women tanning hides. They also expose darker Inuit problems of survival in the modern world.

# Timeline

Each Inuit culture had its own way of recording history. This timeline is based on the Gregorian calendar, which Europeans brought to the Arctic.

**9000 BCE**    Ancestors of Alaska Natives arrive in Alaska.

**2500 BCE**    Ancestors of Inuit migrate across the North American Arctic.

**1741**    Danish sea captain Vitus Bering, sailing for Russia, is one of the first European explorers to visit Alaska.

**1742**    Hundreds of Russian fur traders move to Alaska to obtain sea otter pelts.

**1771**    Moravian missionaries set up the Nain mission station in Labrador.

**1848**    New York whaler Thomas Roys discovers bowhead whales in the Bering Sea.

**1852**    More than two hundred American ships arrive in the Arctic to hunt whales.

**1867**    The US government purchases Alaska from Russia for $7.2 million. Canada becomes a country.

**1898**    Gold is discovered near Nome, Alaska, bringing thousands of outsiders to the Arctic.

**1922**    The film *Nanook of the North* presents an image of Inuit life to moviegoers around the world.

**1954–1957**    Inuit laborers work to build the DEW Line, a string of radar stations that stretched across the Arctic in Alaska and Canada.

**1971**    The US Congress passes the Alaska Native Claims Settlement Act, granting Alaska natives ownership of 44 million acres (17.8 million hectares) of Alaskan land.

**1977**    The first Inuit Circumpolar Council is held in Barrow, Alaska.

**1999**    Nunavut is declared a new Canadian territory.

**2015**    Barack Obama visits the tiny town of Kotzebue, Alaska, as the first sitting American president to visit the Arctic. The warmest year on record is recorded in the Arctic.

# Glossary

**ancestor:** a blood relative from whom one is descended

**baleen:** plates in a whale's mouth that filter food from seawater

**carcass:** the body of a dead animal

**dialect:** a form of a language that is spoken in a particular area and has some of its own words, grammar, and pronunciations

**indigenous:** descended from the original occupants of a land before the land was taken over by others

**language family:** a group of similar languages

**missionary:** a person on a religious mission, especially one to promote Christianity in a foreign country

**parka:** a very warm jacket with a hood

**pelt:** the skin of an animal with the fur still on it

**permafrost:** a thick layer of soil close to the surface that remains frozen year-round in Arctic climates

**prospector:** a person who searches for gold or other mineral wealth

**rudder:** a flat, movable piece of wood attached to a boat to help steer

**sculpture:** art made by carving stone, bone, or other materials

**sinew:** strong tissue that connects muscles to bones

**taboo:** a religious custom that forbids a particular practice

## Selected Bibliography

Freeman, Milton M. R. *Endangered Peoples of the Arctic: Struggles to Survive and Thrive.* Westport, CT: Greenwood, 2000.

McGhee, Robert. *The Last Imaginary Place: A Human History of the Arctic World.* New York: Oxford University Press, 2005.

Struzik, Edward. *Future Arctic: Field Notes from a World on the Edge.* Washington, DC: Island, 2015.

Wright, Shelley. *Our Ice Is Vanishing/Sikuvut Nunguliqtuq: A History of Inuit, Newcomers, and Climate Change.* Montreal: McGill-Queen's University Press, 2014.

LERNER

e

SOURCE

Expand learning beyond the printed book. Download free, complementary educational resources for this book from our website, www.lerneresource.com.

# Further Information

The Arctic Environment
http://www.nwf.org/pdf/Schoolyard%20Habitats/ArcticEnvironment.pdf
Find out more about the Arctic, including its history, landscape, and the effects of climate change.

Canada's First Peoples
http://firstpeoplesofcanada.com/index.html
Read about the history of the native peoples of the Canadian Arctic, including traditional lifestyles, art, spirituality, trade and travel, conflicts, and modern life.

The Inuit's View of Life
http://www.greenland.com/en/about-greenland/culture-spirit/history/myths -and-legends/the-inuits-view-of-life
Check out this website to learn all about the culture and modern life of Inuit in Greenland.

Kallen, Stuart A. *Native Peoples of the Subarctic.* Minneapolis: Lerner Publications, 2017. Learn about more North American Indian nations in this book about native peoples in the subarctic regions of Alaska and Canada.

Orr, Tamara. *The Inuit of the Arctic.* Kennett Square, PA: Purple Toad, 2014. Check out this book to read more about the history and customs of Inuit and their lives in modern times.

Qitsualik-Tinsley, Rachel, and Sean Qitsualik-Tinsley. *Stories of Survival & Revenge from Inuit Folklore.* Iqaluit, Nunavut: Inhabit Media, 2015. Read these stories about Nuliajuk, a sea spirit; Nanurluk, a huge polar bear; and other Arctic beings to learn about Inuit storytelling culture.

# Index

## Photo Acknowledgments

The images in this book are used with the permission of: © iStockphoto.com/Bastar (paper background); © Loop Images/UIG/Getty Images, pp. 2–3; © Laura Westlund/Independent Picture Service, pp. 4, 6; © John E Marriott/All Canada Photos/Getty Images, p. 7; The Granger Collection, New York, pp. 8, 11, 12, 15, 30; REUTERS/Chris Wattie, p. 9; © Marilyn Angel Wynn/Nativestock.com, pp. 17, 19, 22, 23, 29, 40; © Igor Golovnov/Alamy, p. 24; © pilipenko D/123RF.com, p. 25; © Todd Mintz/Nature Picture Library/Corbis, p. 26; © Cindy Hopkins/Alamy, p. 28; © ullstein bild/Getty Images, p. 32; The Granger Collection, New York, p. 36; © Tom Hanson/AFP/Getty Images, p. 36; FLAHERTY/The Kobal Collection, p. 37; © Ronald Karpilo/Alamy, p. 38; © White House Photo/Alamy, p. 39; AP Photo/Mark Thiessen, p. 42 (top); © Fred Hayes/Getty Images, p. 42 (bottom).

Front cover: © Eastcott Momatiuk/Stockbyte/Getty Images.